D1222637

METAMORPHOSIS

by Franz Kafka

ADAPTED BY

DAVID FARR & GÍSLI ÖRN GARDARSSON

OBERON BOOKS
LONDON

First published in 2006 by Oberon Books Ltd.
521 Caledonian Road, London N7 9RH
Tel: 020 7607 3637 / Fax: 020 7607 3629
e-mail: info@oberonbooks.com
www.oberonbooks.com

Reprinted 2008, 2010

Metamorphosis adaptation © David Farr & Gísli Örn Gardarsson 2006

Based on *The Metamorphosis* by Franz Kafka

David Farr and Gísli Örn Gardarsson are hereby identified as authors of this adaptation in accordance with section 77 of the Copyright, Designs and Patents Act 1988. The authors have asserted their moral rights.

A catalogue record for this book is available from the British Library.

ISBN: 978-1-84002-688-7

Cover photograph by Eggert Jónsson

Printed in Great Britain by Antony Rowe Ltd, Chippenham.

CHARACTERS

FATHER

MOTHER

GRETE

GREGOR

STIETL

FISCHER

A Doctor

Lyric

This adaptation of *Metamorphosis* was first performed on 29 September 2006 at the Lyric Hammersmith in a co-production with Vesturport, with the following company:

Nina Dögg Filippusdöttor

Gísli Örn Gardarsson

Kelly Hunter

Jonathan McGuinness

Ingvar E Sigurdsson

Adapted and directed by David Farr &
                              Gísli Örn Gardarsson

Music by Nick Cave & Warren Ellis

Design by Börkur Jónsson

Lighting by Hartley T A Kemp

Sound by Nick Manning

Produced by Kate McGrath of Fuel

SCENE 1

We see two rooms in an apartment in a small mittel-European city in what may be the early twentieth century. Gregor's room is a small bedroom. It is simply but adequately furnished. A bed. A desk. A chair. Some cloth samples on the chair. A bookcase. A sofa. On one wall a picture of a beautiful woman in a fur stole. For now this room is in semi-darkness. The living/dining-room below is where the family eat. It is lined with books and has an effortful civility – lower middle class but fallen on tough times. Pictures, books. Lamp-lit eating table. A door leads to the kitchen. Another door leads out to the building's landing.

Outside it is raining slightly. The sky outside the windows is grey and colourless.

Everybody wakes up. Nobody is going anywhere.

It's a normal morning, a morning of routines. Gregor's FATHER is eating his breakfast, reading the paper. GRETE, Gregor's sister is bringing in the coffee. Gregor's MOTHER is fussing.

Just before the family breakfast begins the FATHER notices a pair of shoes. The FATHER picks the shoes up.

FATHER: Lucy? Come and see.

The MOTHER approaches.

MOTHER: What is it?

FATHER: Gregor's shoes.

MOTHER: What about them?

FATHER: They're still here.

Beat. He shows them to her.

MOTHER: But I don't understand. They can't be.

FATHER: But they are.

MOTHER: But he's left. He leaves at a quarter to five to catch his train.

FATHER: Well his shoes have not left with him.

GRETE: Go and check, mother.

The MOTHER turns to climb the stairs.

MOTHER: Gregor?

She walks up the stairs. GRETE stands in the middle of the stairs, the FATHER stage-left by the dining table. The anticipation is high.

MOTHER tries to open Gregor's bedroom door. She can't.

FATHER: Well? Is he there?

She knocks.

MOTHER: Gregor it's gone seven o'clock. Shouldn't you be at work by now?

Inside, GREGOR SAMSA awakes from bad dreams and finds himself turned into a huge insect. GREGOR is lying legs up in his single bed.

Pause.

Gregor dear?

Downstairs – impatient shouting:

FATHER: Tell him he's missed his train.

MOTHER: Gregor, are you awake?

FATHER: He's supposed to be in the office by quarter to seven.

GRETE: He's tired.

FATHER: We're all tired.

GRETE: He's been working so hard.

FATHER: He should be up by four, out of the house by quarter past five. What on earth is the matter with him?

FATHER bellows:

Gregor Samsa!

GREGOR: What time is it?

MOTHER: Is that you dear? You're terribly late you know.

GREGOR: I'm all right mother. I'm just getting up.

FATHER calls out from the living-room.

FATHER: What's his excuse?

MOTHER: (*Whispering to the others.*) I can't understand him. Are you sure you're all right Gregor? Can I bring you something?

GRETE: Open the door Gregor.

GREGOR: I must have overslept. I had this terrible dream. It's all the travelling, all the train journeys and hotels. I don't sleep. I'm coming now.

MOTHER: What did he say?

GRETE: His voice is not normal. I can't make it out.

MOTHER: I can't understand a word he says. Gregor tell us what's wrong!

FATHER: Is he dressed yet? Get a move on man!

GRETE: Gregor, open up.

GREGOR: The next train leaves at half seven. I can still get that one. I'll have to hurry. Get me some food mother, I'm starving. I mustn't forget my samples. If I go hell for leather, I can make it.

MOTHER: Oh Hermann. I have no idea what he's saying. It's frightening me! Gregor I can't understand you!

GREGOR: I must have caught a chill. It's the hotel bedrooms, they're so draughty in the winter.

FATHER: Gregor open this door!

GREGOR: I'm just getting up now.

FATHER: This is your father speaking. Open this door immediately!

They start to pound against the door. Terrible noise. Interrupted by:

The front door bell rings. The family pause.

Who could that be?

MOTHER: Go and see, Grete.

GRETE: It's a man in a suit.

MOTHER: Someone from his work!

GREGOR: No don't. Don't open the door. Talk to him through the keyhole. Tell him I'm on my way.

FATHER: Gregor stop snorting and open this door.

GRETE opens the front door.

GRETE: Good morning. I apologise for my appearance.

STIETL: Good morning I'm wondering if employee Gregor Samsa is here?

GRETE: He's still in bed.

Pause.

STIETL: In bed?

GREGOR: Don't let him in!

STIETL: My name is Herr Stietl. I head up employee
Samsa's department.

GRETE: Would you like to come in?

GREGOR: I told you not to let him in!

GREGOR falls out of bed.

STIETL: What's that noise?

GRETE: I'm afraid that's Gregor. Something's happened.
Mother this is Herr Stietl from Gregor's work.

STIETL: A pleasure to meet you Frau Samsa. I head up
employee Samsa's department.

MOTHER: He's not himself Herr Stietl. He's not well. It's
the long winter we've been having. You know Gregor
– he never misses a train. Always prompt and well
presented. He's never received the slightest complaint
before. He works all hours. Never goes out. Just stays in
his room, sorting his samples, checking the trains. He
does woodwork. The frame on his wall, he did that, it's
wonderful, you must see it. I'm so pleased you're here.
We can't get him to open the door.

GREGOR: I'm coming now.

MOTHER: And this dreadful noise he makes. He's unwell,
it's the only explanation. A winter cold. A throaty
cough.

STIETL: I'm sure you're right, madam. Although the truly hardworking employee must disregard personal illness for the greater good of the business.

MOTHER: Oh he's hard-working. He works like a...

FATHER: Gregor. Are you going to let Herr Stietl in or not?

GREGOR: No. Not yet.

STIETL: What is he saying?

Pause. GRETE begins to cry.

GREGOR: Who's crying? Is that you Grete? Don't worry, Grete, I'm not going to lose my job for refusing to open a door!

STIETL: Herr Samsa. You've locked yourself in your room.

GREGOR: It's a habit I've developed from staying in hotels.

STIETL: You're not even bothering to talk properly. You're two hours late. I have to say never have I experienced such a brazen dereliction of duty. You're giving your parents a terrible scare. They're sick with worry out here.

GREGOR: (*Who is beginning to get out of bed on to the floor.*) I'm on my way.

STIETL: (*Close to the keyhole.*) We had hopes for you. You seemed a diligent and hard-working type. That's all changed. The MD suspects that your absence may be connected with the authority he recently granted you to carry cash on the company's behalf. I denied it in the strongest possible terms but now I'm not so sure. Your position isn't rock solid you know. People have been asking questions about your performance. All right, no one's bringing in the millions this winter but there's low sales and there's no sales. You hear me Herr Samsa? And no sales is not a word in our dictionary.

GREGOR: Herr Stietl I'm letting you in right now. I came over all light-headed. A dizziness.

STIETL: What's he saying?

GREGOR: Last night I had a sense. Just a sense that something might happen. That I might be laid low. But I thought I'd get over it. And I tell you what Herr Stietl. I will get over it! The eight o'clock train has my name on it.

STIETL: Is this some kind of joke?

FATHER: Dear God what's happened to you boy?

MOTHER: Grete go straight to the doctor. Tell him Gregor is ill. Bring him instantly.

GRETE: Yes mother.

Exit. GREGOR struggles to reach the key.

GREGOR: Those accusations of embezzlement you mentioned are absurd Herr Stietl. I refute them absolutely. I may need a locksmith to help me Grete. And as for the sales figures. You obviously haven't seen the latest batch of orders from my trip East. A bumper crop! An abundance!

STIETL: Listen. I can hear something.

GREGOR is reaching the key.

He's turning the key.

Long pause as he struggles with the key… The family lean in… Unbearable tension.

GREGOR: I didn't need a locksmith after all!

Pause. The door opens. STIETL enters. Stops dead.

STIETL: Ohhh…

He staggers out of the room. MOTHER enters.

MOTHER: Oh my… Oh Greg… Oh God in… Aaaah! Aaaah! Aaaah!

She faints.

GREGOR: Mother?

FATHER: Get back from her. Get back! You…! You…! Oh God. Oh!

He collapses weeping.

GREGOR: I'll just get my samples. I need to find my coat and I can be on my way. It's so cold out. Where are you going Herr Stietl? Shall we travel together? I need you to explain to head office the cause for the delay – a minor affliction, now thankfully overcome. I need your support at this time. I know what they think of us travelling salesmen.

GREGOR has found his legs now and is scuttling out of his room towards STIETL.

STIETL: Get away from me…

GREGOR: Herr Stietl where are you going! Please don't leave without me!

GREGOR grabs STIETL by the legs. A fight in the living-room.

Herr Stietl you have to listen! I know what those offices are like – one late arrival and the gossip begins! 'Samsa was late. Samsa's a glory boy. Samsa's not pulling his weight.' Herr Stietl I am begging you – give me your word that you will stand up for me!

MOTHER enters into the living-room, sees GREGOR. Screams.

MOTHER: Oh God! Help! Help! Help!

…and falls onto the table knocking over the coffee. The coffee pours endlessly over the floor. GREGOR is distracted by this.

GREGOR: Mother? Are you all right?

MOTHER: Get away from me.

GREGOR: Mother please calm down. No Herr Stietl please don't go!

But STIETL escapes out of the front door, slamming it behind him. FATHER is awakened by the sound of the door slamming and enters the living-room.

MOTHER: Stop him. Stop him!

FATHER grabs Herr Stielt's cane as GREGOR turns to see the cane.

FATHER: Oh no you don't.

GREGOR: That's Herr Stietl's cane. He must have forgotten it.

FATHER brings the cane down hard onto the floor. Grabs newspaper and starts to drive GREGOR back to his room like an animal back to its pen.

What are you doing?

FATHER: Hssss! Hssss! Hssss!

MOTHER opens a window in the living-room. The curtains flap, rain pours in, and wind blows papers over the room. She leans out and weeps.

MOTHER: Oh God help us! We're good people.

FATHER: Hssss! Hsss! Hssss!

GREGOR: Father please. You're hurting me.

MOTHER: Honest.

FATHER: Hsssss! Whooaaaraaaaaaagh! Hsssss! Whooaaaraaaaaaagh!

MOTHER: Decent.

GREGOR: I can't go backwards! Let me turn round! I'll go faster if you let me turn round!

MOTHER: We live quiet ordinary lives.

FATHER: Hssss! Whooarrghh! Hsssss! Ha! Ha! Ha! Ha!

MOTHER: Why us? Why us dear God?

GREGOR tries to turn round. FATHER reads this as an aggressive act and beats more furiously.

Oh no you don't! Hssssss! Hssss! Hssss!

GREGOR: Aaaah! No! Aaah! Aaaah!

FATHER: GET Hsssss INTO Hsssss YOUR Hssss ROOM!

He beats him to the door and then as GREGOR tries to get in he closes the door too quickly and squeezes GREGOR.

GREGOR: AAAAAGHHH!

FATHER: GET IN!

GREGOR: AAAAGHHHH!

FATHER: GET…IN…! GET…IN…!

FATHER forces GREGOR into his room kicking him as he is stuck between the door posts. GREGOR rips his jacket as he is forced through the door. FATHER slams the door. He catches his breath leaning his body weight against the door. He walks downstairs, sits stiffly. Sees the coffee on the floor.

MOTHER: I'll make some more.

SCENE 2

GREGOR is in shock in his room. He retreats into a corner, shaking and lies motionless, breathing quite heavily.

Downstairs GRETE comes back home with a doctor.

FATHER, still in shock, sends the doctor away explaining that it was all a big mistake. Doctor exits. FATHER locks the door behind him; they all look at each other. FATHER sits down in his chair. MOTHER gradually finds her way into doing something normal; cleaning some of the furniture etc.

GRETE waters a flower. We feel time passing.

FATHER eventually falls asleep. MOTHER decides to bring milk to Gregor's room. She tip-toes past FATHER. GRETE watches her from where she is sitting.

MOTHER opens the door of Gregor's room. Just a slight crack. She peaks into the dark and gently places a bowl of milk inside Gregor's room. She then shuts the door and runs crying down.

GREGOR wakes up to the smell of milk.

He eventually finds it and tries to drink it. Disgusted by it, he spits it out.

He feels depressed, and in an effort to take his mind off it he crawls back and forth in the room, worried about the discomfort he has brought onto his family.

The door opens. Light through the door. A figure, GRETE, enters. She is terrified.

GRETE: You didn't like the milk? It's always been your favourite.

GREGOR slowly comes out from his hiding place. GRETE sees him, wretches and rushes behind the door. Slams it shut. Then gathers herself, re-enters bravely.

Could you cover yourself please Gregor while I get used to it.

GREGOR hides under a sofa.

Wait.

She leaves, enters the living-room, fetches six more bowls which she balances and brings back to the bedroom.

Vegetables from last night's supper. This is some old cheese we were about to throw away. Meat bones. Raisins and nuts. And here's some bread. I've put butter on this one. And butter and salt on this one. Let's see what you prefer. And this is for your…personal use.

She slides him a larger tray.

GREGOR: Thank you.

GRETE: Try something.

GRETE moves away, barely able to look, maybe even leaves the room. GREGOR comes out from his hiding place. He tries the various foods. The cheese he loves.

You like the cheese.

GREGOR: Yes.

GRETE: But not the bread nor the nuts.

GREGOR: Not so much.

GRETE: Mother and father are asleep. We've sent home the
servants. We tidied the house ourselves. Mother cooked.
But we didn't eat a morsel. No appetite.

GREGOR tries to nudge a chair to get up to the window.

You want me to put a chair by the window? You want to
look out?

GREGOR: At the street.

*GRETE puts a chair by the window. GREGOR climbs onto
it, wincing.*

GRETE: Are you hurt?

GREGOR: Father. Crushed me in the door.

Looks out.

GRETE: You've always hated the hospital being opposite
your window. The trees along the avenue still don't
have any leaves. This winter is never ending.

GREGOR: Why didn't you play the violin today?

GRETE: I can't understand you Gregor.

GREGOR: The violin. You play so beautifully. I want you
to go to the Conservatoire to train. I was saving a little
every week. I was hoping by Christmas to have enough.
I know mother and father don't approve but they would
have come round to our way of thinking in the end.
How will I ever raise the money stuck in this room?
How will I ever get you what you deserve?

GRETE: I find it so hard to understand you.

GREGOR: Try to understand!

GRETE: I feel like, if I really try, I can understand.

GREGOR: I said I want you to play the violin at the Conservatoire.

GRETE: The what?

GREGOR: The violin. The violin. The violin!

Pause.

Grete. You won't abandon me? Will you?

Pause.

GRETE: It's all right Gregor. I'll look after you…

SCENE 3

We are downstairs in the living-room. Everything as if normal. FATHER reading the paper. The doorbell rings. Everyone ignores it. GRETE moves around the room doing everything. MOTHER leaves the house, to do shopping, looking like a spy. GRETE is up and down the stairs with food for GREGOR, cleaning his room, changing the tray. GREGOR moving from the floor to the wall.

All this framed by FATHER sitting reading the paper.

As he finishes we are suddenly at dinner. It's already at the table (has been prepared during previous sequence) but no one is eating. In the bedroom, GREGOR is hanging upside down, listening. During the scene he heads up the wall to listen more.

FATHER: (*Reading in the living-room.*) It says here that due to the extended winter the Emperor's Gardens may not open this year.

GRETE: Have some meat father.

FATHER: I'm not hungry.

GRETE: Mother, you must eat something.

MOTHER: I've had all I want.

FATHER: (*Reading.*) 'The cold winter combined with recent February rain is endangering full budding of spring flora.'

GRETE: You've barely touched it.

MOTHER: You finish it.

GRETE: I don't want it.

FATHER: (*Reading.*) 'Doubts remain over the survival rate of the Emperor's tulips, primula, daffodils, marigolds…'

MOTHER: Hermann you have mine.

FATHER: I don't want any!

MOTHER: Well there you are then.

Pause. MOTHER begins to cry.

GRETE: Oh Mother.

MOTHER: Sorry. Sorry I…

FATHER: Pull yourself together Lucy.

MOTHER: I just feel – it's something I've done. Something in me.

FATHER: Don't be so absurd.

Pause.

GRETE: What if we invited him to join us?

FATHER: What?

MOTHER: What did you say dear?

GRETE: What if we asked him to come and eat with us?

MOTHER: But that's impossible.

GRETE: He's not eating. We're not eating. Something must be done. Neither of you have so much as knocked on his door since it happened.

MOTHER: I've been busy in the kitchen. Your father has been looking into our affairs. And the stress of the whole thing…

GRETE: I know what he likes to eat. We could give him some mouldy cheese and a few rank vegetables. It might make it easier for us to eat our beef and potatoes.

FATHER: It's an absurd idea. To have…that…at the dinner table.

GRETE: I don't see it as so absurd.

FATHER: With your mother's health? She might break down.

GRETE: (*Very innocently, no attack.*) Father. If we don't invite Gregor to the table, what are we going to do?

FATHER: Well I mean to say.

MOTHER: She's right. Bring him down Grete.

GRETE leaves the living-room.

FATHER: You'll regret this. Mark my words. You're more fragile than you think.

GRETE: Gregor. Gregor!

She enters the room. Split-scene here.

MOTHER: We have to try something. All I've been able to do this past fortnight is think about him stuck up there.

GRETE: We want you to come and have dinner with us.

GREGOR: I don't want to.

FATHER: I'm only thinking of you.

GRETE: Please Gregor.

GREGOR: I will be an embarrassment to Mother.

FATHER: The embarrassment!

GRETE: Mother asked you to come.

Pause. GREGOR comes out of his hiding place. GRETE contains her disgust but GREGOR notices.

GREGOR: No I don't want to!

GRETE: It's fine! Come on.

He follows her out of the bedroom and into the living-room

Gregor's coming in now.

FATHER: I want to state very clearly my objection to this.

MOTHER: Hermann!

GREGOR and GRETE enter. Utter repulsion from PARENTS.

FATHER: Oh dear God!

MOTHER: Oh! Ohhh!

GRETE: Mother! It's all right Gregor. Where would you like to eat?

GREGOR goes into a corner.

That's a good idea. Nice and safe there. I'll bring you some old cheese. Would you like some water?

MOTHER: Stop staring at him Hermann. Have some stew.

FATHER: You expect me to eat in this situation?

MOTHER: At least make a show.

GRETE returns with some cheese.

GRETE: There. Your favourite.

She sits. Everyone tries to eat. But can't.

MOTHER: Well this is nice.

Pause.

He's not touching his cheese. He's just staring at us.

GRETE: Sssh, mother. Eat your stew.

MOTHER: I can't while he just sits there!

GRETE: He's waiting for you.

MOTHER: Well you try.

GRETE tries. She can't.

FATHER: This is a grotesque charade.

MOTHER: What we need is a conversation.

FATHER: What conversation?

MOTHER: Winter's lasting forever this year. The buds are barely on the flowers and we're already March. Some say the severe frosts may have accounted for as much as three quarters of the blooms.

She is starting to cry. She tries to eat. Can't.

GREGOR: I want to go back.

FATHER: What did he say?

He starts to go up the stairs.

GRETE: But you haven't eaten anything.

GREGOR: My company isn't pleasing you.

FATHER: What is that awful noise he's making?

MOTHER: Hermann! Eat your food.

FATHER: I can't eat! I can't eat like this! It's degrading!

GREGOR: I agree with father.

FATHER: Oh stop that dreadful din! Get him out of here someone please!

GRETE: Stay where you are, Gregor. Gregor is not leaving.

FATHER: Well fine. Let him stay. I'm going about my business just the same.

He goes to the safe, takes out some papers.

We don't have time for this mockery. We have to discuss our financial position.

MOTHER: Oh yes let's talk about money, it will take my mind off everything.

FATHER: Let's sit this way so we don't have him in our eye-line.

He sits looking away from GREGOR.

As you know the collapse of the family business five years ago left us with substantial debts. Ever since we have been living off of Gregor's earnings. His promotion from junior clerk to travelling salesman was in this sense most propitious. He has been earning enough for the whole family to live on.

MOTHER: But now?

FATHER: The situation is fortunately not as grave as might have been the case. I was able to hold on to some small investments after the collapse of the company.

MOTHER: Hermann, you never told us.

FATHER: These have grown steadily and the dividends have remained untouched. I have also been able to put aside a proportion of Gregor's income for future needs.

MOTHER: That's wonderful. Isn't your father clever, Grete?

GRETE: Why didn't we use that money to pay off our debts? Then Gregor wouldn't have had to work such long hours.

FATHER: I chose an alternative strategy and one which is now bearing fruit. Gregor's condition places the onus on us to find alternative methods of income. This small pot will bide us over until such alternatives are discovered.

MOTHER: But it's not enough for us to live on?

FATHER: In perpetuity, no. For a year or two maybe. But in the long-term… We must work.

GRETE: Work?

FATHER: Yes work. Work will set us free.

Suddenly GREGOR cries out.

GREGOR: But how can mother work with her asthma? She has to lie down after the simplest of domestic tasks. How can little Grete sully her soft hands with hard labour? She should be playing the violin, not slaving away at some menial chore!

FATHER: Will someone get him away from me!

GREGOR: And you father – you haven't worked for five years. What work will you find at your age?

MOTHER: Stop him Grete. He'll knock over the stew.

GRETE: It's always me. Coping with every situation. You haven't either of you looked at him since it all began.

GREGOR: It's all my fault Grete. The shame is on my head.

GRETE: Not so much as popped your heads round the door.

FATHER: You're just taking it out on us because you now realise the absurdity of your idea. Bringing him down here! Taunting us with his presence! Stupid, naïve girl!

GRETE: How can you say that!

MOTHER: Stop it. Stop it both of you!

GREGOR: Don't be upset mother. It's all my fault. But I can solve it!

GRETE: Gregor stop this ridiculous display!

GREGOR: I want to explain my ideas for what to do with the money. You must not work. The money can be wisely invested. I know some high-yield funds that I can get you in touch with. You'd be looking at eight, nine per cent growth plus a dividend…

MOTHER: Aaaah! Get him away from me!

FATHER: Get back!

GREGOR: But I want to help!

FATHER: We have to stop that racket! People will hear. Questions will be asked!

No one moves. Finally it is GRETE who stands angrily.

GRETE: I'm taking you up, Gregor. I'm sorry. It hasn't worked.

Pause.

GREGOR: Yes take me up please.

GRETE: You'll be safer in your room.

GREGOR: Yes please.

GRETE: I can bring you some food later. When you're hungry.

GREGOR: I would like that very much.

MOTHER: My baby.

They head towards the bedroom. Downstairs the MOTHER continues to quietly wail.

GRETE: I'm going to lock the door. Okay?

GREGOR: Yes please.

MOTHER: My baby…

GRETE takes the key from the inside of the room and locks it from the outside.

My poor baby…

The FATHER suddenly erupts

FATHER: That is not your baby!

GRETE walks down and FATHER and MOTHER watch as she puts the key around her neck. They all understand that GRETE now is the guard to Gregor's room.

I do not want to see that in my living-room ever again.

And FATHER storms out.

SCENE 4

Sudden switch to upstairs. GREGOR is finding great joy in exploring his room. He has embraced his insect-ness in full.

Below, MOTHER and GRETE are discussing as GREGOR flies around.

GRETE: He's happier like this.

MOTHER: Let me at least go and see him.

GRETE: It's not wise. It only upsets him.

MOTHER: He's my son. I should be looking after him.

GRETE: He's fine. He's in his own world.

MOTHER: But it's been over a week!

GREGOR: (*Calling out as he whizzes across the ceiling.*) She's right, mother. It's quite wrong for you to enter this room.

MOTHER: I can't deny my natural instinct.

GRETE: You heard what father said. It's better you have nothing to do with it.

MOTHER: I understand the rationale behind what you're saying but my maternal urges say something different.

GREGOR: Listen to what she's saying! It's not right!

GREGOR swings round to intervene. But as he does so GREGOR falls from the ceiling to the floor in his excitement.

MOTHER: What was that? Oh Gregor! Gregor!

GREGOR: I'm all right. Nothing to worry about.

GRETE: I'll check him.

MOTHER: No I will. Give me the key. GIVE ME THE KEY!

GRETE: You heard what father said.

MOTHER: My son may be hurt in there! Give it to me! Give it to me you hussy!

But GRETE doesn't. A moment of real tension between them.

GRETE: We'll go together.

They climb the stairs. Pause. GRETE takes out the key.

Gregor cover yourself up. We're coming in.

GREGOR covers himself up. They enter.

MOTHER: Where is he?

GRETE: Under the sofa. Don't look.

GREGOR: Mother. Is that you? My eyesight – I don't know what's happened to it.

MOTHER: Are you all right Gregor?

GRETE: He's fine mother. He's always jumping off things.

MOTHER: This place is a tip.

GRETE: He prefers it like this.

MOTHER: He may well do but in this house there are standards. What does he do all day?

GRETE: He likes to move around.

MOTHER: There's not enough space. We should make some more room for him. Help me Grete. Help me move the furniture.

GREGOR: But I like the furniture.

She starts to move the furniture out of the room.

MOTHER: This can't be any use to him. It just gets in the way.

GREGOR: Mother what are you doing? That's my bookcase.

GRETE: Just stay there Gregor and stop that noise. Mother doesn't need to see you.

MOTHER: What he needs is space. Clarity.

GREGOR: But I don't want you to move anything.

The WOMEN, with calm but superhuman strength, clear the room. GREGOR watches helplessly.

GRETE: We'll leave the sofa so he can still get under it.

MOTHER: Everything else is going.

GREGOR: No stop please

MOTHER: Poor boy – he doesn't understand what we're doing. We're only thinking of you Gregor.

GREGOR: But I don't want you to take it.

He starts to come out from his covers.

GRETE: Gregor get back!

GREGOR: That's my desk! I did my homework on it at school. And you've taken my bed that I've always slept on and my chair where I put my samples…

The WOMEN succeed in taking out the desk. The room is empty except for the framed picture on the wall. GREGOR goes up the wall and holds on it for dear life The WOMEN re-enter. The MOTHER sees where GREGOR is. She freezes.

MOTHER: Give me the frame Gregor.

GREGOR: No.

MOTHER: Give it to me.

GREGOR: You're not having it! No! No!

MOTHER: Give me the frame. Give it to me. Give it to me! GIVE IT TO ME!

MOTHER has a fit. Collapses.

GRETE: Now look what you've done! You've killed her! Mother are you all right? I'll get some smelling salts.

She exits. GREGOR swoops down from the ceiling/wall and lands near MOTHER.

Mother? Are you all right?

But in his energy he misses MOTHER and smashes into the living-room where GRETE is fetching salts. In horror she splashes some on him. The bottles smash and GREGOR is cut.

GREGOR: Aaaah!

GRETE: Get away from me!

GREGOR: Aaah! Aaagh!!!!

MOTHER: Ohhhh!

32

GRETE: Mother! I'm coming!

GRETE runs upstairs. GREGOR is left in the living-room alone still hanging in mid-air.

GREGOR: No! Noooo! Nooooo!

The door opens. FATHER enters the room in a startling military-style uniform – actually the uniform of a bank messenger. FATHER has some bags of groceries in his hands. He sees GREGOR – in the living-room.

FATHER: What the hell?

GRETE: Gregor tried to attack Mother! She had a fit.

FATHER: What did I say would happen? You women never listen!

MOTHER screams out from upstairs.

MOTHER: Don't hurt him Hermann!

FATHER: You walked right into his trap. And he took full advantage! Well – I'm going to teach you a lesson my boy.

He takes out some of the groceries and starts beating GREGOR with them: melon, meat, eggs, flower, tomatoes, the painting, flowerpots, celery, milk, wine…etc.

I'll teach you to show some RESPECT!

GREGOR flees upstairs, falls down the stairs…etc. Fight all over apartment ending in Gregor's room. GREGOR tries to shut the door but the FATHER foils him.

GREGOR: Aaaah!

FATHER: I'll teach you what respect means!

Stuff embeds itself into GREGOR's skin, injuring him. He is beaten and ends sunk on the floor.

MOTHER suddenly grabs hold of the FATHER.

MOTHER: Stop, Hermann! Save his life. I beg you. Spare him. Spare him! Spare him!

She pulls him out of the room and the door slams. In despair GREGOR starts to crawl insanely over the whole room like a wounded animal, crying, shrieking, reeling, turning…

SCENE 5

GREGOR is in great pain. He crawls around in his room. Shaking.

At the same time we are aware of the family catching their breath downstairs. FATHER pours himself a glass of brandy. Drinks a few glasses. MOTHER dries her eyes. GRETE sits and brings out a book.

The door is open. But GREGOR can't move. He is injured. Downstairs GRETE is learning French. MOTHER is sewing underwear. FATHER is dozing.

GRETE: Michel est mon ami. Je suis l'amie de Michel. Marianne est ma sœur. Je suis la sœur de Marianne. Philippe est mon frère. Je suis le frère de Philippe.

MOTHER: She was so rude when I collected the linen this morning. Treated me like a peasant woman. I've a good mind to sew the legs of her stockings together.

GRETE: Je suis la mère de Solange.

MOTHER: I wanted to say to her. My husband had his own business. If it hadn't been for a quirk of fate, I'd be in your shoes now. You'd be darning my linen!

GRETE: Je suis le père de Pierre et Natalie.

MOTHER: Beautiful necklace she had. And look at the quality of the lace. If she saw the state of this place… I can't keep up with everything. We work all hours of the day. Even you. To think… Even you, little Grete. Slaving away in that store. A common sales girl.

Upstairs GREGOR begins to listen – heads towards the door but it hurts him and he can barely move.

GRETE: Sssh.

MOTHER: Isn't the door shut?

GRETE: I've left it open. It's comforting for him to hear our voices. But he won't want to hear that.

MOTHER: We don't want him coming down. We don't want a repeat of the incident.

FATHER: (*Stirring from his doze.*) He's not going anywhere.

MOTHER: Hermann. Why have you still got your uniform on?

FATHER: Why not? It's such a fuss to change.

MOTHER: You just love the look of yourself in it.

FATHER: What if I do? Should a man not be proud of his work?

MOTHER: But it gets so dirty. I brushed it down only this morning. Look at it now! There's grease on the buttons.

FATHER: Easy to remove a grease stain.

MOTHER: He slept in it last night. In that chair.

GRETE: I think it looks dashing.

FATHER: There you are, Lucy. Listen to your daughter. Herr Gillingsbrucke came up to me today when I was on duty. He's one of the junior bank clerks, a real bright spark. Small chap. Little moustache. 'Get me a bacon sandwich and coffee would you Samsa old fellow.' 'A pleasure to do my duty,' I replied. 'And a pastry for Gruber. And on your way back, post this letter for me, there's a good chap.' 'Yessir!' 'Oh and Samsa,' he said. And then he saluted! Saluted me! Hermann Samsa! Junior clerk Gillingsbrucke! Respect Lucy. Respect.

Smiles all round.

Come here Grete. Come to papa. What are you doing?

GRETE: I'm improving myself.

FATHER: Quite right too.

GRETE: Hermann est mon père. Je suis la fille d'Hermann.

FATHER: Did you hear that Lucy?

GRETE: It's French.

FATHER: Is it now?

GRETE: Lucy est ma mère. Je suis la fille de Lucy.

FATHER: Ha! She'll go far this one. Do another one. Go on.

GRETE: Je suis la sœur de...

Pause.

MOTHER: What is it, dear?

GRETE: Nothing.

They get on with their tasks. FATHER starts to drop off.

This gentleman came in the department store today and asked for perfume for his wife. He sprayed it on my wrist. Put his nose to my arm and took in a deep breath.

Said it would give him a better sense of what he was looking for.

GREGOR gets drawn to the staircase by the discussion he hears about GRETE now having a job. We hardly see him but feel his presence.

MOTHER: Did he buy it?

GRETE: Two bottles… One for his wife and one for his…

MOTHER: Grete! Your father…

GRETE: I don't think he's listening mother.

And indeed FATHER has started to snore. MOTHER sews. FATHER sits in the armchair and dozes. Gentle peace. FATHER half wakes.

FATHER: Is this my life? Is this the peace and quiet of my old age?

Then back to sleep. Now MOTHER starts to get sleepy.

MOTHER: Did you take him his food?

GRETE: Who? Oh – no I forgot. I'll do it in a minute.

MOTHER: Do it now dear.

GRETE: It's such a bore.

MOTHER: I know. I know…

She falls asleep in her chair, in the middle of her work.

Silence for a while. Upstairs, GREGOR starts to scratch at the floor. GRETE hears the scratching.

GRETE goes up.

GRETE: I'm coming in, Gregor. Please cover yourself up, I'm not in the mood.

GREGOR covers himself up.

GREGOR: I'm a little hungry.

GRETE: What are you saying?

GREGOR: I'm hungry. I think maybe you forgot…

GRETE: Really Gregor how do you expect me to understand all that?

GREGOR: You don't have much time for me now. I understand. You have to work so hard.

GRETE: I'm going to bring you some food okay? Just stop hassling me.

GREGOR: You shouldn't be working in a department store.

GRETE: What?

GREGOR: My sister should not be working in a department store.

GREGOR says this vehemently. Angry. GRETE is angry now.

GRETE: Don't you start getting angry with me! You presume too much, Gregor. I look after you. I feed you each day… I clear up after you.

GREGOR: Don't give up on the dream of the Conservatoire. You haven't played the violin for a month! All this talk of work breaks my heart.

GRETE: That's enough! Understand that your position in the house has changed. You no longer have the rights of an individual family member. You are unable to fulfil the responsibilities that give you those rights. You are still our brother and son, but the nature of that relationship has evolved.

GREGOR: That you, my sister, should even consider, on my account of giving up all those dreams forever. Because of me!

GRETE: I can't understand a word you say.

GREGOR: You said you could understand if you tried.

GRETE: What are you saying?

GREGOR: No don't. Try and understand! Please – keep trying!

GRETE: Oh for God's sake Gregor!

GREGOR: You're not trying! Please try.

GRETE: All I can hear is noise. NA NA NA NA NA NA.

GREGOR: It's not noise, I'm speaking quietly now.

GRETE: You're doing it again. NA NA NA NA. It's killing my ears.

GREGOR: But I'm scarcely speaking.

He is speaking so quietly now.

GRETE: STOP THIS AWFUL NA NA NA NA NA NA. YOU'RE DRIVING ME INSANE!

This very loud. Pause. Now quietly.

I have to go.

GREGOR: Don't go.

He starts to uncover himself.

GRETE: Get back – don't look at me!

MOTHER wakes in the living-room.

MOTHER: What's going on in there?

GRETE: Disgusting!

This violent, but she stops because GREGOR shits.

Oh my God.

GREGOR: I had no idea.

GRETE: Oh…

GREGOR: An accident.

GRETE: The smell. I can't stand it.

GREGOR: I'm not in control of my functions.

GRETE: I bring you a tray. Every day I bring you a tray! I clean your tray!

MOTHER: (*In the living-room still, but overhearing, weeping.*) This has got to end. This has got to end!

GREGOR: Don't…

GRETE: That's it. I…

GREGOR: Don't give up on me!

But she has gone, slamming the door behind her. GREGOR weeps and bangs at the door but in vain.

SCENE 6

Sudden new energy as the MOTHER leaps up and starts preparations. Sister is changing, or making herself beautiful. FATHER also leaps up and fusses, clearing the living-room and taking stuff out of the room.

MOTHER: Imagine the difference it will make to us if he takes it. Thirty crowns a month.

GRETE: He won't take it unless it looks perfect. He has so many options.

MOTHER: I can't wait to see him.

GRETE: Oh you'll like him mother. He's everything you'd want in a lodger. He's just been promoted from junior manager of the haberdashery division to assistant senior manager. He's only been there two months. The store has great hopes for him.

MOTHER: I've been trying to picture him.

GRETE: He rows at weekends.

MOTHER: Strong shoulders.

GRETE: And runs the steeplechase. And is, they say, top swordsman in the Sports Society.

MOTHER: I hope he doesn't try any swordplay in our living-room!

They laugh, slightly over the top.

GRETE: He's from a decent family in the East of the country but has come here to make his own way in business. He's going to achieve great things.

MOTHER: A decent family. Oh Grete.

GRETE: Of course he's just a lodger.

MOTHER: Yes he's interested in coming purely as a lodger. Of course he is. But nonetheless…

They hear a scratching.

GRETE: Nothing can go wrong tonight. This is too important. Nothing can be left to chance.

She runs up the stairs. Enters the room. Efficient. Clinical.

Gregor you are not to appear tonight. Is that clear?

Pause.

You do not leave this room. You do not utter a word. You do not make a sound. Utter silence do you hear me. Tonight you do not exist.

GREGOR: But Grete…

GRETE: No don't start all over again.

GREGOR: …I don't feel very well… I need food…

The doorbell rings.

GRETE: Will you be quiet!

Downstairs FATHER enters in a panic.

FATHER: One of my buttons has fallen off.

MOTHER: Oh Hermann how could you!

GREGOR: I feel faint.

GRETE: Shut up! Shut up!

FATHER: I was trying to do it up. The damn thing wouldn't go in the hole!

MOTHER: I told you to stop wearing it in the house.

The doorbell rings again.

GREGOR: Grete…

GRETE: All right, that's it. I have HAD ENOUGH!

And she grabs some curtain, ties him to it, gags him and closes and locks the door. GREGOR is alone. Meanwhile…

FATHER: Is there time to sew it on?

MOTHER: Of course there isn't time!

FATHER: What should I do?

MOTHER: Leave it. We'll say that I'm polishing them one by one.

GRETE runs down.

GRETE: Father pull yourself together!

The doorbell rings. Upstairs GREGOR raises his head from the floor.

I'll go. No you go mother. It will be more appropriate.

MOTHER: I can't go. I'm shaking from top to toe. Hermann!

FATHER: Why me?

GRETE: Will one of you answer the door!

They both go to answer the door.

FATHER: Let me!

MOTHER: Well go on then!

FATHER opens the door.

FATHER: Welcome!

FISCHER: Herr Samsa.

FATHER: Hermann. Please call me Hermann. And you are Herr Fischer.

FISCHER: It is a pleasure to meet you sir.

GRETE: Let him in, father.

FATHER: Of course. This is my wife.

FISCHER: Of whom I have heard a great deal. May I say what a pleasure it is to meet you.

MOTHER: Herr Fischer how delightful to meet you. May I take your coat.

FISCHER: Thank you.

MOTHER: Come through. Come through. Such a soft material. Is it yak's wool?

FISCHER: I don't think so.

MOTHER: No of course but it's so…so…

She dances with the coat.

GRETE: How was your journey Herr Fischer?

FISCHER: I caught the tram as you suggested. I had a slightly longer wait at the stop than anticipated.

FATHER: I must apologise.

FISCHER: It's not your fault.

FATHER: No but for such a personage…to wait at a tram-stop for what must have felt like hours…

FISCHER: It was barely seven minutes.

FATHER: Seven minutes. Did you hear that, Lucy? I once waited for a tram for something close to nine minutes. It was at Fruhlingsplatz. A lady sitting next to me at the stop started to tut beneath her breath. Tut tut tut. And I must say, Herr Fischer, hearing your story tonight, I feel disposed to do the same and damn the tram company say I! Tut tut tut Herr Fischer!

GRETE: A drink Herr Fischer.

FISCHER: Maybe prior to settling in I ought to see the room? It would be presumptious of me to accept your hospitality before we were sure that our business was successful.

MOTHER: Yes of course. I'd quite forgotten. The room Hermann.

FATHER: This way Herr Fischer.

He inexplicably stands to attention and salutes.

FISCHER: Your uniform…

FATHER: I work for the city bank Herr Fischer. I am honoured to fulfil a modest duty in that respect. A small but significant cog in a great machine.

MOTHER: If you're wondering about the button, it's being polished.

Pause.

GRETE: Shall I show you the room.

FISCHER: Thank you Miss Samsa. May I say how beautiful you look tonight. Is that a new dress?

GRETE: Please call me Grete. This way.

They exit.

MOTHER: He's remarkable.

FATHER: Quite the sort of man I was hoping for. He possesses an inner steel. I recognised it instantly.

In the room above, GREGOR is weak but listening.

MOTHER: I just remembered. She never took up his food.

FATHER: Whose food?

MOTHER: His food.

FATHER: Well you can't do it now.

MOTHER: But we forgot yesterday too.

FATHER: Lucy at this moment we must focus on what is at hand. And what is at hand is Herr Fischer, a month's rent in advance and a potential…

MOTHER: Hermann!

FATHER: … friendship with Grete. Nothing must poison the purity of that aspiration.

MOTHER: How strong you are.

Enter FISCHER and GRETE.

FISCHER: The room is most acceptable, Herr Samsa.

MOTHER: Do you think so?

FISCHER: I am able to pay a month in advance if that is satisfactory?

FATHER: Most satisfactory!

MOTHER: Oh Herr Fischer. I'll get cooking straight away!

FATHER: Let us have some wine to celebrate!

She enters the kitchen.

FISCHER: Herr Samsa. Let me give you the money.

FATHER: Oh please don't concern yourself with trivial matters such as money now.

FISCHER: I would prefer to conclude our business.

He counts out the notes.

FATHER: Well…that's extremely good of you Herr Fischer.

He hands the money to Hermann but is looking at GRETE.

Thank you. Thank you Herr Fischer. Thank you.

FISCHER: And now we can enjoy ourselves.

GRETE: The wine, father.

FATHER: Of course. In vino veritas!

He beetles off to get the wine.

GRETE: I'm glad you liked the room.

FISCHER: Its simplicity appeals to me. I hate pretension.

GRETE: It's not much of an apartment I know. I hope to move out when the opportunity arises.

Beat.

I often look at you with the customers at the store. Always so courteous, so professional.

FISCHER: I don't know how long I shall be there.

GRETE: Oh no?

FISCHER: I am considering joining the army.

GRETE: Oh Herr Fischer…

FISCHER: I believe there will be nothing more important in the coming years than the defence of one's country. There are wars on the horizon and every able-bodied young man must do his duty. I don't come from a rich home…

GRETE: No…

FISCHER: But I believe I have the capacity to lead. To be an officer.

GRETE: Oh you do.

FISCHER: I have been watching you Grete across the shop floor. You have a quality I very much like. A devotion to duty.

They approach each other. Enter FATHER.

FATHER: The wine!

FISCHER: May I congratulate you sir on the excellence of your home. Never have I felt so comfortable, so welcome. A home reflects the man who leads it.

FATHER: Well I do what I can. Let us not pull our punches Herr Fischer. Times have not always been easy.

FISCHER: No sir they have not. It takes stamina and resolve, to struggle through what arrows fate sends us. It takes guts. Your health sir!

FATHER: Your health!

FISCHER: I look at this house and I see a family that is about to blossom. Like a flower not yet fully opened.

FATHER: (*Deeply moved.*) That's exactly what we are. Isn't it Grete?

FISCHER: It has survived the harsh winter and when those petals open, when the thick aroma of its stamen is allowed to release, then, sir the world will swoon!

FATHER: It's remarkable the way you understand us. We are poor of course…but we work hard…

FISCHER: In a nutshell Herr Samsa! Work! Energy! I rowed five miles of river this morning. Then I worked all day. Am I tired? No of course not. Energy is a moral quality. The decadence of our society stems from a lack of energy. When I watch your daughter on the shop floor, so limitless with her generosity, serving all comers! That's energy. Where others shrink from the challenge of service, she stands up and is counted!

FATHER: That's my Grete.

The MOTHER has entered.

MOTHER: The meal will be a few minutes.

FISCHER: The smells promise great riches.

MOTHER: It's just a simple prime cut of beef…fresh today…

FISCHER: I prefer my beef unadorned. I hate fussiness in food. Or in anything for that matter. I see now where you get your beauty Grete.

MOTHER: Oh Herr Fischer. You embarrass me.

FISCHER: Forgive me. I spoke without thinking.

FATHER: And so you should. Everyone should be free to speak without thinking! We worry so much, we're penned in by our anxiety. My wife is beautiful! My daughter is beautiful!

FISCHER: Why be ashamed?

FATHER: Precisely! There's something about you Herr Fischer. I feel free for the first time in ages… It's like a weight has been taken from my shoulders.

MOTHER: Well how shall we pass the time before dinner?

FATHER: I know! Grete. You must play for us! Do you like music Herr Fischer…?

FISCHER: Um well…

FATHER: Oh you must hear Grete. We're very keen for her to attend the Conservatoire. But recently she hasn't touched the instrument.

GRETE: I've been too busy. Anyway Herr Fischer doesn't want to hear me play…

FATHER: Of course he does, don't you Herr Fischer?

Beat.

FISCHER: Why not?

FATHER: There you are!

GRETE: He's just being polite father.

FATHER: Nonsense. Herr Fischer doesn't need to be polite here.

FISCHER: Not at all. Play, Miss Samsa. It won't take long and then we can eat.

GRETE: All right.

She exits.

FATHER: That's my girl!

FISCHER: Herr Samsa. Hermann. Now that I have paid in advance, I wonder if might stay tonight? I had a temporary solution which has fallen through…

FATHER: Of course. The room is yours. Stay tonight, tomorrow night. Stay as long as you like!

FISCHER: Do you shoot, Hermann?

FATHER: I never have.

FISCHER: I'll take you to the Lodge. Filled with only the finest men, young and old. Men together. I could nominate you.

FATHER: Me?

FISCHER: We go out beyond the river. In high season there's no amount of excellent prey. I can teach you the techniques…it's all in the cock…

FATHER: Here she comes!

GRETE enters.

FISCHER: The speed with which a man can move from readiness to the trigger depends on the speed of the cock. The elbow must be flexible but alert.

GRETE: Let Herr Fischer finish, father. It's much more interesting…

FISCHER: And then the speed of the reflex!

He performs the cocking action in the room.

And in seconds your prey is dead on the ground. DA! DA! DA! He didn't see a thing!

Pause.

FATHER: Shall we listen to Grete now?

FISCHER: What? Oh yes. Sure.

GRETE starts to play. A sad slow liede. Her playing is hesitant but oddly beautiful. Immediately GREGOR is up listening.

GREGOR: Grete?

Downstairs FISCHER finishes his glass. He speaks over the music.

FISCHER: Chance of another glass old man?

FATHER: Of course.

He quietly pours.

FISCHER: I can smell your beef Frau Samsa.

MOTHER: You must be hungry Herr Fischer.

FISCHER: After five miles on the river? I could eat a live calf.

They laugh. The playing continues, sad, sweet. GREGOR is crying, fighting to get the curtain gag off him.

GREGOR: She's playing so quietly. I can't hear it. I can't hear it.

GREGOR starts to scratch slowly at the floorboards/walls. He pulls up a floorboard. Then another. It makes a slight noise.

FISCHER: Did you hear something?

A pause in the playing.

I thought a heard a noise. Like a scratching.

FATHER: I didn't hear it.

MOTHER: Play some more, Grete dear.

GRETE starts to play again. GREGOR unpicks more floorboards. He is weeping, trying to get closer.

GREGOR: What's happened to my ears? I still can't hear it. I can't hear it!

More noise can be heard below.

FISCHER: There's definitely something going on up there.

FATHER: Keep playing, Grete. I don't think it's anything.

FISCHER: That's not nothing Herr Samsa!

FATHER: Just rats maybe.

FISCHER: You have rats? Why haven't you exterminated them!

FATHER: Not us. Next door.

FISCHER: But the noise is not coming from next door Samsa! It is coming from here!

MOTHER: Lovely playing, Grete. Play some more.

She plays on. GREGOR rips more floorboards and then lies close to the floor. FISCHER stands.

FISCHER: Damn it Samsa. There's something going on up there. I intend to investigate.

FATHER: There is nothing going on.

FISCHER: Let me through, Samsa.

MOTHER: Please Herr Fischer sit down.

FISCHER: I do not appreciate being lied to.

FATHER: There is nothing going on! There is nothing going on! THERE IS NOTHING GOING ON!

This with intense, murderous violence. GRETE stops playing. Beat.

MOTHER: (*With a smile.*) Sit down please everyone. The meal is ready!

At which point GREGOR smashes through the floor and hangs from the light fitting above their heads.

Chaos on stage. Screams.

FISCHER: What the hell is that?!

Pause.

GREGOR: I will get you to the Conservatoire. I will get you there.

MOTHER: Grete, take Herr Fischer to his room would you?

GRETE: Yes of course. This way Herr Fischer.

FISCHER: Not until you've told me what that is!

FATHER: Just go to your room please Herr Fischer.

FISCHER: Herr Samsa! I have been invited into your house! I have been lied to! I haven't even had my supper! I demand an explanation!

FATHER: Just go to your room!

FATHER starts to force Herr FISCHER out of the living-room.

FISCHER: Herr Samsa. I must insist you stop pushing me.

FATHER: Please Herr Fischer go to your room and in five minutes all this will be sorted out!

He and GRETE attempt to push Herr FISCHER out of the room. FISCHER, however, performs some kind of martial art on them and they are thrown to the floor. MOTHER collapses in an asthmatic attack.

FISCHER: Herr Samsa! This depraved and disgusting assault on my sensibility is unforgivable. Unforgivable! I am handing in my notice on the spot! It is too late now for me to find alternative accommodation for tonight but in the morning I shall pack my bags and leave! I do not expect to be charged for the night's board. I do not expect to see or speak to any of you in the future. You may expect litigation to follow, for damages suffered against my person and to my dignity whilst under your roof and in your care! I took you for a great man sir, for one of the new generation! I have been sorely deceived! Good night to you sir – and to your kind!

GRETE: But Herr Fischer.

FISCHER: Out of my way – shop-girl!

And he leaves to go to his room chased by FATHER. FATHER and GRETE return into the room. Silence.

GRETE: Father, mother…let me speak.

FATHER: But Grete…

GRETE: Let me speak. It is now clear, if ever there was any doubt, that we cannot continue like this. I won't utter the name of my brother in front of this…this… creature…so all I'm going to say is this. We have to get rid of it. We've tried looking after it, caring for it. We invited it to our table, then when that didn't work we tried to let it live its own life in a space adapted for its own needs. But that didn't work either. Nothing works. We've done everything in our power, no one could argue with that.

FATHER: Hear hear.

MOTHER: Oh God…

She has a slight asthma attack. GRETE rushes over, holds her.

GRETE: It will be the death of you, mother. I can see it. We've worked ourselves to the bone, we've suffered endless agony…we've sacrificed EVERYTHING, ALL OUR HAPPINESS. We can't… I can't take any more.

MOTHER: But darling Grete – what can we do?

Pause.

GRETE: We have to get rid of it. That is the only solution. We all have to remove from our minds any idea that this thing is Gregor. How can it be Gregor? If it was, he would have realised long ago that human beings can't live with such a creature, and he would have left of his own will. We wouldn't have a brother but could at least preserve his memory. But this…this organism persecutes us…haunts our every move, drives away all hope of redemption. See what it has done to Herr Fischer! Our ticket out of here! Can't you see it wants to drag us to into the gutter, into the shit, yes into the shit beside it! Well I won't go! (*Violently to GREGOR.*) I won't go, you scum! You cancer! (*To MOTHER and FATHER calmly.*) We have to exterminate it. Get it out.

MOTHER: She's right.

FATHER: Yes. She's right.

GREGOR turns to GRETE.

GRETE: It's doing it again. Stop it father!

FATHER picks up a carving knife for the meat and brandishes it above GREGOR. But GREGOR just holds out his hands to GRETE helplessly.

MOTHER: No wait.

GREGOR: You're right Grete. You were always so clever. It's time for me to disappear. Time for me to. Tmmm frrrr mmmmm tttttt dssssspppppprrrrrrr. Ddddssssppppprrrr.

GREGOR is just moaning now. We are at last hearing what the family hear. Now GREGOR turns sadly and begins to leave the room.

MOTHER: It's going…

GREGOR turns and unbelievably slowly make his way back to his room, unlocks the door, enters and closes it behind him. In the room he slowly sinks, sinks into a motionless pile. All the time he makes these appalling strange noises.

GREGOR: Ddddddddsssssspppppppprprrrrrrr. Dddddddsssssppppprrrr. MMNNNNN. NA NA NA NA NA NA NA NA NA NA NA NA.

Until at last he is silent and still.

Downstairs, MOTHER and FATHER both collapse into chairs. GRETE stands like a sentry over the living-room. Music here – GREGOR's death.

Night turns to day. Now GRETE starts to climb the stairs. She enters the room and sees GREGOR dead.

She picks something up and pokes it at GREGOR. He is lifeless. She pokes again. GREGOR falls down from where he is hanging like a piece of meat.

She pokes him where he is lying. He is completely lifeless.

GRETE: Mother? Come up please.

They enter the room and stand over him for what seems to be quite a while.

MOTHER: Is he…?

GRETE: Yes.

She prods him again.

FATHER: Well. Thanks be to God.

GRETE: He looks so thin.

MOTHER: He ate so little.

GRETE: And when he did eat, it came straight out the other end.

Pause. MOTHER, FATHER and GRETE all come together. Close in on each other.

FATHER: Lucy, Grete. We need some time alone. Alone together.

Herr FISCHER has entered the downstairs room.

FISCHER: Herr Samsa! Frau Samsa! I am waiting for my breakfast!

Pause. The FAMILY do not move.

This is beyond a joke Herr Samsa. I require my breakfast and my deposit to be returned to me.

Pause.

I warn you Herr Samsa. I have friends in the Grand Lodge. They are considering me for initiation to Permanent Member status. You do not want Herr Fischer to be your enemy.

Pause.

Last chance Herr Samsa. Or you will find your family's name on lists you would rather it wasn't.

The SAMSA FAMILY, as one, start to descend the stairs. They stick firmly together. From the staircase.

MOTHER / FATHER / GRETE: Get out of my house.

FISCHER: What exactly do you mean by that?

MOTHER / FATHER / GRETE: I mean what I say. There's no breakfast for you here.

Pause.

FISCHER: Very well. If you will please return my deposit.

Pause. FATHER throws the money on the floor.

FISCHER: You insult me sir.

FATHER: I intend to.

FISCHER: Pick it up and hand it to me.

FATHER: You want it. You pick it up.

FISCHER: I will not pick it up!

GRETE: Pick it up, tailor boy.

They all stare at him. Slowly he picks it up.

FISCHER: You will regret this action most deeply. Most severely you hear me. The time will come when we will clear the vermin from the cesspit that passes for our society. And you are on the list.

He leaves but forgets his coat.

MOTHER: Don't forget your coat.

He grabs his coat and leaves. The FAMILY show palpable relief. Emotion etched on their faces.

Beat. The FAMILY returns upstairs to Gregor's room. They look at his body.

GRETE: We can't leave him here…

MOTHER picks GREGOR up without fuss and puts him in a bag. MOTHER calmly wraps GREGOR up.

MOTHER: Down behind the old tenements there's a narrow ditch. It's dark and out of sight. People are always dumping old mattresses. Broken cookers. Someone threw in a dead work-horse. They say the rats and worms ate it in one night.

As MOTHER speaks there is a transformation to outside. The family dump GREGOR in the ditch amongst the old cookers and discarded rubbish. Pause.

FATHER: I've been thinking. That apartment is too big for us. We should find somewhere smaller. We should make a change.

Pause.

MOTHER: Your father has been saying for a long time that we should move apartment.

FATHER: We'll leave this week. Find somewhere new. Somewhere nearer the centre.

GRETE: Near the department stores.

FATHER: I can walk with you on my way to the bank.

GRETE: Within a year I'll be in charge of my own counter.

MOTHER: Grete. You've turned into a fine-looking young woman. Hasn't she Hermann?

FATHER: She has.

MOTHER: Looking at you now – it's time you found someone…

FATHER: Someone deserving of you.

GRETE: I'm sure that once we've moved. It will be easier. I never liked that place.

MOTHER: It wasn't our choice.

GRETE: We know who chose it…

The body lies below.

FATHER: I tell you what! But how could I have forgotten?

MOTHER: Forgotten what?

FATHER: The Emperor's gardens! They're open from today! The first day of spring!

He grabs the newspaper and reads.

'Contrary to previous fears the blooms of the castle gardens are of unparalleled beauty and fragrance.' We could go and visit them!

GRETE: What about work!

FATHER: We can call in sick!

GRETE: Oh father.

FATHER: Just this once! Live a little, Grete! It won't do you any harm! And we can find a new apartment on our way home!

GRETE: I suppose. I love the gardens in spring.

MOTHER: And it's a beautiful warm spring day.

GRETE: All right then.

MOTHER: (*To GRETE.*) I can see the colour coming into your face. Like a red bloom opening.

FATHER: Come on! The gardens are already open! (*He reads from his paper.*) 'Expect bountiful display of genista, hyacinth, tulips, daffodils, chamalaucium, convallaria…'

MOTHER: How handsome you look Hermann!

FATHER: '…speedwell, toothwort, celandine, anemone…'

GRETE: Wait for us father!

FATHER: '…creeping buttercup, white deadnettle, davidia involucrate, magnolia soulangana, indica azalea and the white willow. The Emperor opens the gardens for the delight of all citizens!'

And suddenly the apartment is gone and we are in the Emperor's castle gardens surrounded by flowers. The FAMILY walk amidst the flowers. And GRETE suddenly steps forward and with all the expectation of youth, stretches her fine young body to the sun.

As she does, GREGOR's body in the ditch starts to be eaten by the rats.

The End.